HAMSTERS

MICHAELA MILLER

Contents

Words in bold, **like this**, are explained in the glossary on page 23.

Wild ones

Wild hamsters live in **deserts**. They sleep underground in **burrows** during the day to keep out of the sun. At night the desert cools down and hamsters come out to search for food.

wild hamster

The most common pet hamster is the golden hamster. All pet golden hamsters came from one golden hamster family found in the Syrian desert in 1930. This is why they are also called Syrian hamsters.

HAMSTER FACT

Hamsters store food in pouches in their cheeks.

3

The hamster for you

Golden hamsters like to be alone. If you put two in one cage they would probably fight and kill each other. Chinese or Russian hamsters will not do this if they are introduced to each other when they are very young.

Russian hamster

HAMSTER FACT

Long-haired hamsters need **grooming** every other day.

golden hamster grooming itself

Hamsters are naturally very active at night and sleepy in the day. It is unkind to keep disturbing your hamster during the day.

Where to find your hamster

A vet may be able to give you the name of a local hamster breeder. **Animal shelters** are often looking for good homes for hamsters. You may even have a relative or friend who has some hamster babies.

When you collect your hamster, take a box with holes in it so that the hamster has some air.

HAMSTER FACT

Hamsters live for about two years.

A healthy hamster

Choose a plump hamster with soft, glossy fur. Its skin should be free of any sore patches, cuts, pimples and rashes. Its eyes, nose, ears, mouth and bottom should be clean.

HAMSTER FACT

Hamsters can catch colds and flu from people.

A hamster crouching in a corner of the cage is probably not well.

Safe hands

Your hamster may not be very tame at first. It may try to wriggle away. Start taming your hamster at night when it is likely to be awake.

Put some food in the cage and tap the front gently to attract the hamster's attention. When it moves forward, hand it some food and stroke it gently.

After a week try lifting the hamster in the palms of both your hands. Do not hold the hamster more than 20 cm above the ground.

HAMSTER FACT

Hamsters will jump and fall if they are frightened.

Feeding time

A good pet shop will have the right mixture of grains, seeds and nuts for hungry hamsters. Hamsters also like fresh fruits and vegetables like apples, pears, tomatoes, lettuce and carrots.

HAMSTER FACT

Rhubarb leaves, potato tops, tomato leaves and **coltsfoot** will poison your hamster.

Feed your hamster once a day — usually in the early evening. Put the food in a heavy dish so that it can't tip over. Attach a **drip-fed water bottle** to the side of the cage and keep it topped up with fresh water.

13

Home sweet home

Hamsters are very busy animals so their home should be as big as possible. It should measure at least 75 x 40 x 40 cm and be made of hardwood. There should be a nest box inside with soft hay or bedding.

Hamsters need lots of exercise, so fix a solid wheel — available from pet shops — to the cage wall. The cage should be somewhere warm but out of direct sunlight and draughts.

HAMSTER FACT

Hamsters need a hardwood gnawing block to wear down their teeth.

Keeping clean

Put a layer of coarse sawdust or **peat** on the cage floor and then kitchen paper, hay and sawdust. Every week clean the cage thoroughly and put in fresh sawdust, paper and hay.

Russian hamsters

HAMSTER FACT

Newspaper and magazine print is poisonous to your hamster. Do not use this to line the cage.

Take away hamster droppings and uneaten food every day. Move some of the **urine**-soaked sawdust to the same corner every day, well away from your hamster's food. It will soon use this area as its toilet.

At the vet's

Hamsters are very healthy animals if they are looked after properly. If your hamster seems to be ill, take it to a vet immediately. Small animals can get very ill very quickly.

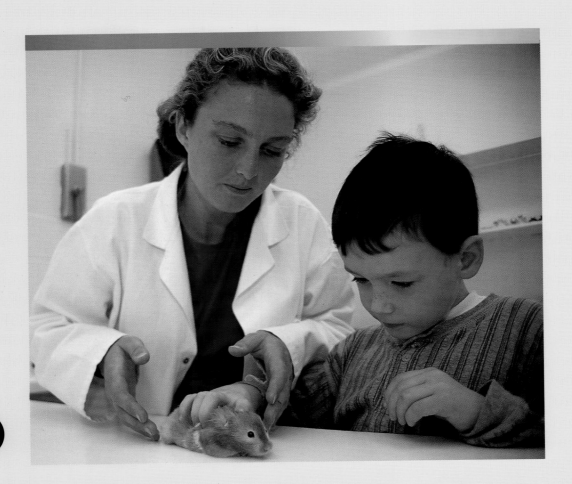

If your hamster's breathing seems strange and its eyes become cloudy, it may not be well. Sore spots on its skin or damp patches around its bottom are also signs of illness — see a vet immediately.

HAMSTER FACT

If your hamster gets too cold, it may hibernate and look as if it is dead. Warm it in your hands before you worry.

19

No more babies

It is not a good idea to let your hamster have babies. A female hamster usually has between five and seven young in each **litter**. Within two months each hamster needs its own cage otherwise they will fight.

HAMSTER FACT

It takes sixteen days for a baby hamster to grow inside its mother.

If your hamster gives birth, leave the mother and babies completely alone except at feeding time, and ask your vet for advice.

baby hamsters — seven days old

A note from the RSPCA

Pets are lots of fun and can end up being our best friends. These animal friends need very special treatment – plenty of kindness, a good home, the right food and lots of attention.

This book helps you to understand what your pet needs. It also shows you how you can play an important part in looking after your pet. But the adults in your family must be in overall charge of any family pet. This means that they should get advice from a vet and read about how to give your pet the best care.

Why not become a member of the RSPCA's Animal Action Club. You'll receive a membership card, badge, stickers and magazine. To find out how to join, write to RSPCA Animal Action Club, Causeway, Horsham, West Sussex RH12 1HG.

FURTHER READING

I, Houdini **by Lynne Reid-Banks**

Glossary

animal shelters   also known as centres or homes. There are lots of these shelters all around the country which look after unwanted pets and try to find them new homes. The RSPCA has about 40 animal centres in England and Wales.

burrows   underground holes and tunnels

coltsfoot   a garden weed with large leaves and yellow flowers

desert   sandy and rocky places in the world where there are very few trees and plants because there is little or no water

drip-fed water bottle   a bottle which is specially made so that the water comes out drip by drip

gnawing block   something for a hamster to chew on to wear down its teeth

grooming   gently brushing your hamster with a soft toothbrush

litter   hamster babies are born in groups called litters

peat   soil used on the bottom of the cage

urine   hamster's wee

Index

First published in Great Britain by Heinemann Library, Halley Court, Jordan Hill, Oxford OX2 8EJ, a division of Reed Educational and Professional Publishing Ltd

OXFORD FLORENCE PRAGUE MADRID ATHENS MELBOURNE AUCKLAND KUALA LUMPUR SINGAPORE TOKYO IBADAN NAIROBI KAMPALA
JOHANNESBURG GABORONE PORTSMOUTH NH CHICAGO MEXICO CITY SAO PAULO

© RSPCA 1997

Designed by Nicki Wise and Lisa Nutt

Illustrations by Michael Strand

Colour reproduction by Colourpath, London

Printed in Hong Kong / China

01

10 9 8 7 6 5 4

ISBN 0 431 03368 4

British Library Cataloguing in Publication Data
Miller, Michaela
Hamsters. - (Pets)
1.Hamsters - Juvenile literature
I .Title II . Royal Society for the Prevention of Cruelty to Animals
636.9'3233

Acknowledgements
The Publishers would like to thank the following for permission to reproduce photographs.
Ardea/ pp6, 16, 20 John Daniels, 21 I R Beames; Dave Bradford pp3, 7, 8, 10-12, 15, 17; Bruce Coleman/ p2 Jane Burton OSF/ pp5 G I Bernard, 9 Zig Leszczynski; RSPCA/pp18, 19 Tim Sambrook

Cover photographs reproduced with permission of: RSPCA

Our thanks to Ann Head and her pets; Pippa Bush, Bill Swan and Jim Philips for their help in the preparation of this book; Pets Mart for the kind loan of equipment; the children of Oaklands Infants School.

Every effort has been made to contact copyright holders of any material reproduced in this book. Any omissions will be rectified in subsequent printings if notice is given to the Publisher.